From Broken to Dearly Beloved

KATHY KING-BOYD

Kathy King-Boyd
From Broken to Dearly Beloved

Second Edition Published by Spines Publishing Platform
ISBN: 979-8-89691-366-5

From Broken to Dearly Beloved

Table of Contents

Introduction

In the beginning, before the typical dating age, I started dating at 15, which is way too early because your brain isn't fully developed at that age. My mother, as an educator, used to say, "Our brain isn't fully developed until around age 25." So, at 15, I lacked sense and experience—about ten years of it—and my life reflected this through years of failed relationships and, as I got a little older, even a short marriage that ended in divorce.

First, I would like to give special honor to my wonderful parents! My beautiful sister and dear brother and I had a great upbringing! With two parents who had their master's degrees and were both educators, who did their best to set us up for success, I am very grateful! They were as nice as could be, and I love them dearly!! May they both, and my beautiful big sister "Rest in Heaven"... and special love to my awesome big brother!!

So, what I'm sharing is based on my personal decisions and the direction of my life, in which the Lord allowed me to experience and go through for purposes He saw fit, way after I left home. He brought me from hopeless situations to hopefulness after later being abused, traumatized, misused, taken for granted, and taken advantage of in some relationships. You may say, "Wow, Kathy, that's very negative!" No, I'm being truthful and sharing a testimony of what God can do with our brokenness. Through Jesus's love and faithfulness, He healed me a lot and restored my self-worth. Then, Jesus sent me a wonderful husband who was just for me!

Sounds like a fairy tale, huh? Well, it's not. This is a true story involving real people who also witnessed the hand of God in our lives. I didn't mention anyone's names except for mine and my husband, Marvin's. Respectfully, I would have had to get permission from each person, and time would not permit that... but, if you're in here you'll know where you are in our story. And I want each of you to know that, I'm honored that the Lord had you in our lives as He was blessing us! Thank you! And much love to each of you!! It's a story of how I went from brokenness to healing, being loved by a wonderful man who loved God and was faithful to Him first, who adored and loved me, and was faithful to me for almost 41 years of marriage until the Lord took him Home.

But I want to say first that Jesus became my husband spiritually, and He led the man of my dreams to me. He's no respecter of persons and will do the same for anyone! Just follow the signs, tips, and principles for His will in your life—whatever your purpose!

CHAPTER 1

Brokenness In My Past

My early life and challenges reflect the struggles I faced after leaving home, which included heartache and hardships caused by betrayal, loss, and trauma. These experiences left me feeling broken, both emotionally and spiritually.

I received Christ through a tract I got when I was 18, during my first year at Colorado State University in 1972. While leaving the student center, a young Caucasian woman handed me a pamphlet, which I took to my car and read.

It said, "Heaven and hell are 18 inches away. You can have God in your mind, but you need Him in your heart, and there's 18 inches between your mind and your heart." So, since God was just in my mind, I immediately asked Jesus to come into my heart, and I noticed something real and unexplainable happening within.

But, I did not have any Christian follow-up or leadership in college after that happened, so I still wasn't fully committed to Christ and continued to sin and do my thing. But I did notice that I started drawing away from some worldly things I was doing, though not all.

After I finished my first year in college, I returned home, and in the summer of 1973, while back home in Denver, I felt a strong urge to go out to California... and though I did go for my second year of college before classes got started... I was planning on partying first (which shows a lack of commitment to Christ).

But, almost when I first got out there, I was asked to go to a church... I went, and the rest is history! That's where I learned of my salvation and what it entails through Jesus Christ. And how that feeling I felt when I asked Him to come into my heart (in my first year of college) was a real person in all of His glory that really did come in!

The experience I had at that church in California was a powerful one, and I was on fire for God and filled with His Holy Spirit! There were many young people there, and we learned to pray and fast... and we loved and supported each other. We also had a dynamic pastor who taught us the word of God... and it was really a wonderful church.

I spent about seven months in California before returning to Denver. When I got back home to Denver, I had the opportunity to pray with my mom, and she re-dedicated her life to Jesus!! She had received Christ as a teenager and was about 45 years old at this time.

Upon the Lord coming into her life, He also healed her from Lupus which her doctor diagnosed that she had. As her healing manifested by the grace of God, her doctor gradually took her off the medications that she was on;

because she no longer needed them. After all this, my mom lived for another 50 years! All praises to our great God!! She was 95 years young when the Lord took her Home on April 3rd, 2024. My beautiful mother was buried one month later, on May 3rd (her 96th birthday), where my wonderful dad, who was a veteran, had been buried on her birthday 41 years earlier. The Lord was gracious through it all! And so, back to my story... 50 years earlier, when I got back home from California in 1974, I also had a chance to talk with some of my dearest friends and share with them the love of Jesus. Some of them already knew Jesus, and some gave their heart to Him, also! Thank God for His wonderful love!!

Though I gave my heart to the Lord, I was still a woman and desired a husband... not just for sex, but also for companionship and friendship. I had found a nice church, and after a while, one of the brothers and I started seeing each other, and we ended up getting married.

But let me say this: before I got married, I whispered to the Lord, "If it's not your will for me to marry this brother, let me know," But to be honest, I knew in my heart that I was going to marry him regardless of what I felt God might have told me. I'm just being honest... and later, I saw how disobedience and independence from God both were still in my soul, and that is why our soul must also be redeemed, not just our spirit.

Now, let me share some thoughts with you about our spirit and our soul. Our soul comprises our mind, emotions, and our will. Even though I had received Christ and He was in my spirit; as human beings, we are a spirit, we have a soul, and we live in a body. And our spirit is dead because of the sin that Adam and Eve, our foreparents, committed.

> *"For I was born a sinner– yes, from the moment my mother conceived me."*
>
> — PSALMS 51:5 NLT

And when we receive Christ, our spirit comes alive and is redeemed because Jesus died for us (and that was the price to be paid for our redemption). So by believing in what He did and accepting/receiving Him into my heart (remember in the car in college?!) my spirit was saved (redeemed) as Jesus had pleased God and paid the price for me (by dying on the cross, and God the Father raising Him from the dead)... and Jesus' righteousness is what God looks at when it comes to His forgiveness and acceptance of us! And this is true for any and everyone who receives and believes in Him and in what He did! And my soul was and is yet being saved... because our soul is the part of us that still needs to be transformed, as it is where sin resides —where disobedience and independence from God exist.

Notice where we have a lot of our trouble as humans... our attitudes (anger issues, etc.), lust (sexual issues, etc.), hatred/unforgiveness (entanglement, psychological issues, etc.)... and notice that all of those issues or sins are in our mind, our emotions, or in our will (i.e., our soul). It will literally take a lifetime to be in the process of overcoming all of that. That's why no one can judge another, nor should they, because your issue may not be my issue... but you have one... or should I say we have some.

That's why we need a Savior! To save us from our issues, our sins. But our soul also has good things within it... so let's not be too hard on ourselves. In this world our bodies are vulnerable to sickness and disease. Therefore, it's important to take care of ourselves because these bodies can be affected by illness, and sometimes, people die earlier than they normally would have because of sickness or disease.

Also, keep in mind that we will yield our body to either the issues in our soul or to Jesus/Holy Spirit in our spirit— if He is there. And that will determine our choices and/or our behavior, whether they be good or bad. Just know that Jesus was beaten for the healing of our whole being (spirit, soul, and body), even before He was crucified, (killed) on the cross for our sins. The healing in our soul and our body can come spiritually, or by a miracle, progressively, medically, psychologically etc., or the Lord taking us to Heaven for our ultimate healing!

Hear His word on this:

> "He was wounded for our transgressions, He was crushed for our wickedness, [our sin, our injustice, our wrongdoing]; the punishment [required] for our well-being fell on Him, and by His stripes (wounds) we are healed."

> — ISAIAH 53:5 AMP

And none of us are totally there yet, but CHRIST paid the ultimate price... and this promise is for all of us!! Not religion... but SALVATION (Sozo; to make whole/deliver) and for a RELATIONSHIP!!

Hear God's word:

> *"Now may the God of peace Himself sanctify you through and through [that is, separate you from profane and vulgar things, make you pure and whole and undamaged – consecrated to Him – set apart for His purpose]; and may your spirit and soul and body be kept complete and [be found] blameless at the coming of our Lord Jesus Christ."*
>
> — I THESSALONIANS 5:23 AMP

My husband and I wrote a book about this, called "BodyGuard," to help people better understand it, and see what's really going on and why. You can get through everything, no matter what, and the more you understand your make-up, the more you'll understand how to overcome the hard things concerning it! You can purchase the book for a reasonable price.

Anyway, when we receive Christ, our spirit becomes born again. We must continue to feed our spirit and our soul with the word of God and also continue being filled with His Holy Spirit in order to continue our born-again experience. You may ask, "How is this done?" Read the word of God (the Bible), ask God to help you understand it, and ask Him to continue to fill you with His Spirit. This is important because Jesus said, *"No one can see the kingdom of God unless he/she is born again."* —John 3:3, (paraphrased). Being born again is our spirit becoming alive (through Jesus coming in) and us overcoming in our soul (through God's word, which is still Jesus). And then, *"presenting our body before God as an offering ..."* — Romans 12:1 (paraphrased). So we can yield to His Spirit (say yes) and please Him. Then we can "re-present" (represent) Him to the world in our walk. As Ephesians 4:24 in the Message Bible says:

> *"...take on an entirely new way of life --a God-fashioned life, a life renewed from the inside and working itself into your conduct as God accurately reproduces His character in you."*

And this is not anything we can do on our own... we need the help of a Savior, and He is that help!! A real Person indeed!! His Holy Spirit! And it's a must to receive His help! And He will become our Lord as well!! Not just our Savior!

Now, back to my story... unfortunately (I'm ashamed to say), but that marriage lasted only about seven months before it ended. I felt bad because I believed that, as a Christian woman, I should have had more success in my marriage than that. This failure added to my sense of brokenness. However, I finally realized that I wasn't a failure; I had just experienced a failure. Don't let your failures define you—you are 'not' what happens to you! Remember that! I left that church, and my mother and I started going to a church together. I enjoyed the Lord and getting to know Him in a very personal way. I realized that since He knew everything, I needed to be as honest as I could with Him, and that established my loving relationship with Him even deeper. That is key! I have maintained that sense of reality to this day, and looking back, I realize it has helped me have a wonderful relationship with Christ by always being real with Him. He has blessed me tremendously in so many ways because of that. No, not because I am perfect, but because He is!!! And since He knows every-thing anyway, He loves it when we trust Him and His love for us enough to be truthful with Him. Remember, He is a real person! Just as we prefer our friends or spouse to be honest with us, which we call "being straight-up," it helps us to trust them more. The same goes for Jesus Christ—or Holy Spirit. They are true Beings/Persons like we are human "beings"; they are Spiritual "Beings"—The Father, the Son, and the Holy Ghost/Spirit.

I enjoyed that church as well as worshiping with my beautiful mom, but I longed for more spiritually. She stayed there (and by this time, she was established in the Lord, and had many wonderful relationships with others that helped her enjoy her new spiritual family as well!). So, I started attending another church with young people closer to my age. My pastor there aligned more with what I was used to, from the pastor I had in California. I loved the church and the young community there. We were on fire for God there also; our pastor would sometimes have us praying all night and would bring in revival speakers. It was a wonderful time in my life.

Some years spanned between each time I went to another church, but I always had this hunger for more of

God... not ever wanting to just be religious. But looking back, I wish I had approached things differently at times, and I might have avoided the downward spiral of my life at certain times. As I remember, a prophet was coming to Tulsa, Oklahoma, and I wanted to attend his conference.

And I did go. But this is what my pastor's wife asked me before I went, "Did you pray about it?" There's that prayer again... and I told her *yes* because I had prayed about it. But in my mind, I was still going to go, regardless of what I thought may have been what God might have said... Of course, God would want me in a life-changing conference, right?! Not really... if it really was not His will for me to go. And not that the Lord wouldn't have wanted me to be blessed through the conference, but that He would have wanted me to be safe, among other things. He's a Father (and our Heavenly Father at that)! Yes, I went anyway, and it was another big mistake I made that cost me dearly. So yes, pray, but listen and wait to make sure of the Lord's leading or not. So again, in my soul, it showed disobedience and independence from the Lord in my life. And when that happens, trouble awaits us. And that's what awaited me in Tulsa. The conference was pretty good, but pale in comparison to what I went through afterward. I should have returned home to Denver, but I didn't. I stayed there, and I ended up for a brief time being homeless, having no plan. I ran into a man (or I should say... I crashed into a man relationship-wise) who ended up being very abusive and who caused me a lot of pain.

I thought I was in love with him, but it was a terrible relationship, and further in the relationship, he almost choked me to death... literally. After about seven months, I remember going on a three-day fast, and I prayed, "Lord, if this is my husband, please let me know before this fast ends." Foolish, I shouldn't have had to fast to realize that any man that treats you like that shouldn't be your husband! But I guess sometimes love can blind you (or is that just an excuse?!).

Anyway, on the 3rd day of the fast, I remember walking downtown to the library, which wasn't that far... and I saw one of the sisters there who became my friend while in Tulsa. She was a Jewish sister and was very nice and respectful, and we would talk about the Lord. And on this particular day, she had no idea that I was fasting, and she wanted me to try some kosher meat.

So, it being the last day of the fast, I decided to walk with her to a little cafe up the street and try some of this kosher meat. As we turned the corner near the cafe, she suddenly began to prophesy to me right there on the street (I didn't even know she was prophetic!). And she said, "God is sending you a husband, and he shall be faithful to the Lord!" Praise Jesus, that was my answer!! And, the man I was with (whom she did not even know) was not faithful to God. So, God had given me my answer... right before the fast ended! Hallelujah!! He's not just a faithful Savior; but a wonderful Lord!! A covenant relationship with Him is so important to our well-being! He will never leave or forsake us! No matter what condition we're in, and I was definitely in a broken condition. He said,

> "I am with you always [remaining with you perpetually—regardless of circumstance, and on every occasion], even to the end of the age."

— MATTHEW 28:20B AMP

So, with that answer from the Lord, through the woman of God... I began to distance myself from the man that I was with. And the Lord opened the door for me again. I went to a place where I could pray all night, as that was what I was accustomed to doing. One of the pastors allowed me to pray in his church. And while at the altar, I cried out to God and made an intentional decision to let go of the man (from my soul) that I had been with. I took his ring off my finger and placed our pictures on the altar. After praying for a while and falling asleep at the altar, that morning, I woke up and began to pray again. And the phone rang in the church (it was there in the hall). So I got up to answer it, and it was the dear older lady who knew this pastor, who had dropped me at the church, who was trying to help me... and she said that I had a job waiting for me to be a live-in care-giver for a 92-year old elderly lady... so hallelujah, that's just what I needed, so I could get away from the person I had been with and from the city! Again, the Lord showed His faithfulness and His goodness! But notice, I had to surrender that part of my life to God first... and then He moved for me by opening that door! You see, not too long after I had let go at that altar, and the altar of my heart... the phone rang with an answer from God! And, thank God, the Lord rescued me and kept me from possibly being killed... and I never saw that man again! God had delivered me! That's a part of salvation in every way, shape, and form. And the Lord eventually got love or lust for him out of my soul... and the bondage of soul-ties was broken with him!!

So, the kind woman who had been helping me came and picked me up. She took me to the elderly lady's house in another small town in Oklahoma, where I stayed and took care of her. It was a wonderful blessing to have that opportunity, and I was still healing from the harsh life and abuse of my previous relationship. Nonetheless, I was in the process of getting my life right, but I still felt hurt and like a failure... as things were not working out for me in my relationship with men (even though I was careful to just have a few of them, throughout my early life). I had experienced abuse, trauma, and even a divorce, and God knew that I desperately needed healing. He placed me with this elderly lady, and through her, another deliverance was on the way. She asked me to drive her to a tent revival in Muskogee, and I was glad to do so.

I must admit, at this time, I missed those good old red hot services that I used to attend! They were incredibly powerful. So, we went to a revival in a small tent on some land in Muskogee—praise God! I met some of the most beautiful people of God. They were sincere, loved God, and were on fire for Him! They were young adults around my age at the time (about 22, 23, or a bit older). Once again, the Lord had provided me with a path to the saving of my soul; and healing. He's good like that! A friend indeed!! And a compassionate Father! No matter what we go through as humans, He is always there to help us out, no matter who we are (and it helps to ask Him)! He wants so badly to show how much He loves us in an individual way, according to each of us personally, in whatever it is that we're going through! You may not have endured the harshness that I did, but He loves you regardless! On the other hand, you might have gone through way more than what I experienced, but He died for you, too, and "no pit is so deep that He is not yet deeper still!" As said by the Dutch Holocaust hero and writer, Corrie Ten Boom. We kept going to the revival, and eventually, things changed for the elderly mother. So, I was out of a job. And I loved these people. So, the Lord made a way for me to stay there in that part of Oklahoma for a while. And we had tremendous services and mighty moves from God. The Lord used that to bring more restoration in my life as well.

I still struggled with small sins here and there, (remember sins in the soul, nothing really small about them though), but thank God, He was helping me heal from men; I needed strength and healing in my heart from all the trauma I had experienced. So, I continued to dedicate myself to prayer, as that had been instilled in me and was what I knew. The Lord, through His mercy, continued to work in my life... and I learned a powerful lesson about God's grace.

I stopped judging people for their sins, recognizing that I had fallen short and had my own sins to overcome. I had to pray hard and repent myself. This experience taught me that the same mercy God showed me was extended to others also, so I stopped judging others. It was a significant shift in my perspective, especially since deliverance had come so easily when the Lord first came into my life years before.

I stopped smoking and drinking easily and was living wholeheartedly for the Lord. However, after these experiences, I found myself struggling with some of the same issues/sins again, and I had to call on the Lord for help... for real! And even though God helped me overcome some things, it was much harder at that time and I realized that the devil was really trying to destroy me. But God wasn't having it; and wouldn't let him! Instead, the Lord used those experiences that I got myself into... He used them to teach me some hard lessons and mold me into a person that; He could love others through. Hallelujah!

So no matter what you're going through, remember that it could always be worse; just trust that the Lord will bring you through it. Yes, this too shall pass! Trust JESUS!! Keys that I learned are to follow His principles (in His word), pray, confess your sins (be honest with Him no matter what or how degrading things are) and believe (have faith that He hears you and will answer; because He will)... trust and listen to His Spirit (learn His voice, He will teach it to you), and read your Bible (if you don't understand the King James Version, get another version, or translation). There's the New King James Version, New Living Translation, Amplified Version, New International Version, Message Bible, English Standard Version, and many more. Find a Bible that you can understand; the word of God is that important; for the renewing of our mind (remember, our mind is a component of our soul). And the outcome is part of our salvation.

Through all this, the Lord gave me such love for people and souls because of everything I had endured and from which God helped me escape (and literally saved me from!). I kept overcoming challenges and grew stronger spiritually, immersing myself in the word of God by reading and studying it. I realized that my dedication didn't mean I was great; it meant that I was greatly in need! Before these experiences, I had some self-righteousness in me. But, after these experiences... I came to understand the profound truth that Jesus is my righteousness!!! Only because of Him do I live and receive blessings!!

We have to discipline ourselves; that's what being a DISCIPLE means—being a disciplined one. A true Christian is a Disciple of Jesus; I learned that the hard way. Something that can help us understand discipline is the Olympics that were held in Paris (July 26th, 2024 - August 11th, 2024). There were so many talented individuals, and the Bible even uses examples of how athletes discipline themselves to win their medals. We, as believers, must discipline ourselves to win our Eternal Crowns. The word of God says,

> *"Do you not know that in a race, all the runners run [their very best to win], but only one receives the prize? Run [your race] in such a way that you may seize the prize and make it yours! Now, every athlete who [goes into training and] competes in the games is disciplined and exercises self-control in all things. They do it to win a crown that withers, but we [do it to receive] an imperishable [crown that cannot wither]."*

— 1 CORINTHIANS 9:24-25 AMP

Wow, the Olympians are some wonderful individuals

in their field, and we can learn a lot from them. And I'm so happy for all those who did well, and for those who will have another opportunity to do better in the future.

Getting back to our story, none of us in this life have it all together, nor will we until those of us go Home to be with Jesus. So, don't condemn yourself;

> *"God didn't go to all the trouble of sending His Son merely to point an accusing finger, telling the world how bad it was. He came to help, to put the world right again. Anyone who trusts in Him is acquitted; anyone who refuses to trust Him has long since been under the death sentence without knowing it. And why? Because of that person's failure to believe in the one-of-a-kind Son of God when introduced to Him."*

— JOHN 3:17-18 MSG

Remember, no one is better than you! They need Jesus just as much as you do. So, don't be hard on yourself. He loves you just as much as He loves them and just as much as He loves me. But He does want us to discipline ourselves and be strong in HIM!! And we can only do that through His grace, with His help, and in yielding to Him so that He can strengthen us!

So, once again, God made a way, and it was glorious and wonderful. I ended up moving again and went down to Brownwood, Texas. I had come full circle (so to speak) because the prophet who had the conference in Oklahoma that I had gone to a good while back had a church in Texas. He was an older Caucasian man of God, and there were glorious church services there, also. I remember going to the church to pray all night one night (again, something God had led me to do at various times in my life, not because I was so great... but greatly in need). And I was on one side of the church, in the back, praying. I didn't even know the prophet was there until I heard him praying; and we were the only ones in this large sanctuary. As I prayed, I could hear him as he was approaching me because he was still praying... and he laid his hands on my head and began to pray for me.

He said, "God bless this faithful daughter of yours, give her the desires of her heart, and bless her with a husband that will love her." Praise God!! The Lord let me know that He saw all that I had gone through and endured, all of the brokenness, and through His mercy, He was going to change things... as He continued to change me! And I learned through all of this, as we are graced to seek after the Lord, that He will lead and guide us to our healing and deliverance. Through the Message Bible in Ephesians 2:7-9, it reads,

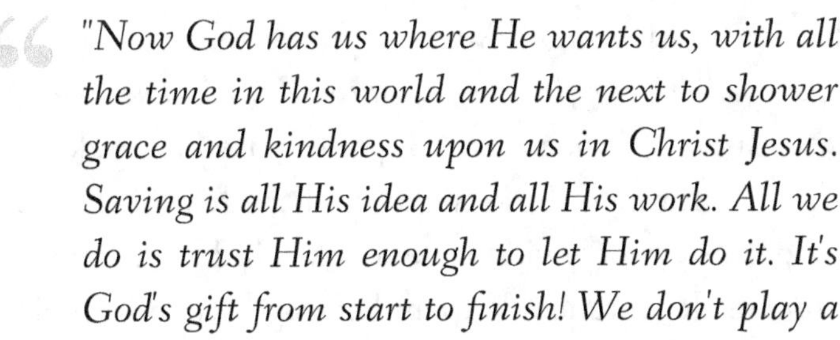

"Now God has us where He wants us, with all the time in this world and the next to shower grace and kindness upon us in Christ Jesus. Saving is all His idea and all His work. All we do is trust Him enough to let Him do it. It's God's gift from start to finish! We don't play a

major role. If we did, we'd probably go around bragging that we'd done the whole thing! No, we neither make nor save ourselves. God does both the making and saving."

So, remember, since *"it's by grace through faith, and not of ourselves, it is the gift of God"* —Ephesians 2:8 (paraphrased), we can always be honest with our Heavenly Father... because He knows anyway. That's how I was delivered before this incident of the prophet praying for me... (about a year before that) I was delivered the second time from cigarettes when it was so hard for me to quit this time... I said to the Lord, and again was honest with Him, "Lord, my flesh likes it, but I know it's wrong and not good for me; please give me the mind to want to quit." And that's exactly what He did! Make note that for some reason, I asked for the "mind" to want to quit (remember, the mind is in the soul, and that is where the struggle was). And I loosely say, for some reason... Well, I know now, the reason to ask for the mind to want to quit is because the Holy Spirit knew that's where my battle was, and He led me to pray and ask the Father for the exact thing that I needed to win that battle! Hallelujah!!

Literally about a week after that prayer, God gave me the mind to want to quit through a scripture I was reading at the time, which said, *"Put away from me the evil of your doings; though your sins are as scarlet, I will make them as white as snow"* —Isaiah 1:16-18 (paraphrased). I could hear God's voice through those words, and the fear of the Lord gripped my heart (conviction), and my mind knew that was my time of deliverance (help and strength)... and I took it!

And this time, I threw the cigarettes in the trash can and haven't touched a cigarette since! And thank God that was now about 48 years ago! The Lord is good, and He's worthy to be praised! He will give you grace and strength in whatever it is you need to do or stop doing! Believe that! Smile's! No matter what you're going through or bound by, Jesus is really a deliverer!! He wants to bless us and lead us to our promised land. He can set us free from not only cigarettes, but drugs, sexual addictions, and anything else we need to be free from! And free we must work toward, because one day we will all stand before God, and if Jesus is not our Representative, and we have not allowed Him to work in our life, there are one of two places we will spend eternity (one is Heaven, and one is hell). Not to scare you, but to share with you the importance of receiving Christ and allowing Him to work graciously in our life!! Read on!

CHAPTER 2

Faith that Works by Love

There are steps to faith. The first step is to establish a relationship with God, and it's not religion. To do that, the Bible tells us what faith is not.

It is not feelings, and faith is not being presumptuous (an adjective meaning "excessively bold or forward. Presumptuous describes someone behaving in an entitled or overfamiliar way and therefore coming across as rude or arrogant." [Definition through Scribbr; Eoghan Ryan, Revised on March 13th, 2023].

Hebrews 11:1 KJV tells us,

> *"Now faith is the substance of things hoped for, the evidence of things not seen."*

It's a firm foundation that makes life worth living. And remember, honesty is crucial. You have to believe and be honest with yourself and with God. And regardless of how embarrassed you may be, trust that Jesus is with you and in you and truly loves you! He's in your heart now. And if not, ask Him in. It's so simple; it's not a big religious ritual you have to perform. Just simply ask... (in your own words), "Lord, please come into my heart, and save my soul!" He loves you more than you could ever imagine or understand. If you had been the only person on this earth who needed salvation, Jesus would have come and died just for you. I'm not loved more than you are! What He's done for others, He'll do for you. And if you're tired and angry, you've got a friend in Jesus. Faith is the key, and it works by love, but it requires effort on your part (it's organic, spiritual effort). It is not the effort where you try so hard; it's the effort where you simply believe, you yield... just like when we're driving, and we're at a yield sign, you know the other person has the right of way... and you yield, you allow them to go before you. So, it is in life, we believe God has the right of way... so we allow Him to go first (to have His way).

That's yielding, or you trust. How? Accept! Yes, when you accept Jesus and simply receive His grace or strength... The real Jesus honors that and comes in to help (like He did when I was in my car in college), and I simply asked Him to come into my heart. Simple! And remember, I said that I actually felt something? I really did! He simply came in. He's a person, and it's as simple as if you're inviting someone into your house; they don't struggle to come in. You're inviting them, you're welcoming them, so they just come in! Right?! Simple! How much more is a person as great as God going to do this simple and beautiful thing?! Yes, it's so beautiful to Him that it delights Him that you would take out the time to ask Him. It shows Him you believe in Him, and that really pleases Him, fam... it really does! And it's not a hard thing to do.

> *"Faith without works is dead being alone"* or, as another translation puts it, *"faith by itself, if it is not accompanied by action, is dead."*
>
> — JAMES 2:17, KJV & NIV

John 3:15b-16, MSG says,

> *"...it is necessary for the Son of Man to be lifted up—and everyone who looks up to Him, trusting and expectant, will gain a real life, eternal life. This is how much God loved the world: He gave His Son, His one and only Son. And this is why: so that no one need be destroyed; by believing in Him, anyone can have a whole and lasting life."*

In my story, you'll notice that every time I received a blessing, deliverance, or breakthrough, it was because I acted on a word or a discipline, such as praying all night or fasting... or when the word said to put away the evil of my doings when it came to the cigarettes. Doing these things didn't make me righteous, but the faith to do them pleased God and showed Him that I believed in His goodness, truth, and love... which in turn brought results. I simply yielded. As it says in Hebrews 11:6 AMP,

"But without faith, it is impossible to [walk with God and] please Him, for whoever comes [near] to God must [necessarily] believe that God exists and that He rewards those who [earnestly and diligently] seek Him."

And it's what we need to continue to do.

So, moving along with my story... After the prophet had prayed for me in Brownwood, Texas, I stayed for a while there in the city... and then went home to Denver for my mother's birthday, which was coming up on May 3rd, 1978. While I was there, I attended a revival that started on July 10th, 1978.

He and I had been the best of friends from kinder-garten to junior high school (now called middle school). We were so close that he used to call my mother "Mom." He thought my friends were cute and wanted to go through me to get to them. It didn't work, though, because they were my friends, and I cared about them. I knew he was gaming, but he and I were still close friends.

Anyway, now redeemed... he happened to be the first cousin of my soon-to-be husband (Marvin Boyd). But nothing was planned other than the plan of God. There wasn't anything in the making because my husband and I had both been married to someone else before, but neither of us was married at this time. So, with nothing in my mind other than wanting to attend a good revival and support them, I went to the revival.

They were both very powerful men; they loved the Lord and were real... and the Lord was using them mightily to preach the gospel! They were both natives of the streets before coming to Jesus—my husband was an OG (an Old Gangsta, and what that entails) before the Lord got a hold of him... and his cousin was a pimp, drug dealer, and a; hustler, {and what that entails), before he was saved. They were both deep in the streets, BUT GOD!!! They both had praying mommas, the kind that don't play! And God heard the prayers of their mothers' and their grandmother! And they had some praying aunts, uncles, and cousins too! And wow! What great preachers they both became! Not only did they become awesome, powerful preachers through years of healing and deliverance themselves, but they also became some of the greatest men and men of God that I knew or knew of!

What God can do when you turn it all over to Him... He's faithful like that! He was faithful to their praying mothers, and He was faithful to those broken men! Well, I got one of those OGs, and oh boy, what a man, what a man... Whatta mighty, mighty good man! Hallelujah! Won't God do it! Yes, HE WILL!!! Smile's! And mommas, and grandmommas don't give up on your children! We hold onto the horns of the altar on their behalf!! And God hears our prayers!!! Believe that!!

Anyway, back to the revival service, I sang a song during the testimony service, a-cappella. Marvin told me (later, after we were married) he remembered hearing singing. He was in the back, reviewing his notes, and thought it was me... and after putting his notes away, he came out to get ready to preach and saw it was indeed me. I finished my little song; it wasn't like I was a songstress or soloist or anything like that. I just felt led to sing a stanza or two of a song that was composed by some close friends of mine called "Saved by Grace." Which later ended up being just one of my husband's favorite songs. I finished and sat down, and once the testimony service was over, they introduced Evangelist Marvin Boyd to preach. And my, my, my, I'll never forget his message, "I Want to Know HIM [JESUS]." And man, did that brotha preach! I wanted to know Jesus even more; it was powerful! It was so anointed, and I was so blessed through it! I received that word and kept saying, "Lord Jesus, I want to know you. I want to know you." That was the desire of my heart. Truly, I wanted to know Jesus in a greater way, even through all my weaknesses, brokenness, sin, and everything I had done and been through. I still wanted to know Jesus! After the sermon, he had an altar call and invited us to come forward if we wanted to know Jesus in a greater manner.

I went to the altar, as we were raising our hands and praying... and I got down on my knees, and again, I was crying out to God for Jesus to come in, save, heal, deliver, and help me! Crying out... "I want to know you, Jesus!!!" I wasn't thinking about nobody but Jesus and receiving more of Him! I was calling on His name!! And, (again, as a side note... after we got married), Marvin told me that when he saw me down on my knees, crying out to God like that... hallelujah, he said that he pointed to me and said, "God, that's the kind of woman I want! A woman who prays like that wouldn't hurt me." Praise God!! I had no idea! My attention was on Jesus, but God was setting things up!! Hallelujah! And He was about to answer some prayers! The prayers of the prophet that prayed for me, and of course, my many, many, prayers asking the Lord for a good man and husband! Smile's!

After that powerful service was over, we were all so blessed. I had two close friends that I was giving a ride home from the revival, which started on a Sunday morning. So, after service, my friends and I left, and as I was about to drive away, we saw Marvin (whom we called Brother Boyd) coming out of the door of the church... he saw us and came over to the car because he knew all of us. And he greeted us... and we said hi and how blessed we were in the service. He thanked God and us... and then said that he was going to go pray for a couple of sisters the next day and asked if we wanted to come.

We believed in praying. We were young women on fire for God. And God through his mercy had restored the fire in my soul after all the brokenness and pain that I had gone through and endured. And all three of us said yes, that sounded good. So, we were all planning on going, and it just so happened the next day when Bro. Boyd came to pick me up; my other two friends couldn't make it. So, I was the only one who ended up going. So, it was just he and I. We went and prayed for the sisters (one was in the hospital, and one was at her home). We had a wonderful time of prayer with each sister! And looking back on that experience of prayer time, it was as if the Lord was setting Marvin and me up to work ministry together! Which we did after marriage, we prayed and loved on people for almost 41 years! Hallelujah!! Anyway, he brought me home, and we began to talk in the car. He told me that he saw my ex-husband in Dallas just a little while back and found out that we weren't married anymore, so we talked a little about that. And I asked him about his wife, and he said they weren't together anymore either.

So, we finished our talk, and we prayed, and I went inside. And things started happening from then on... even though we weren't trying to make things happen... we ran into each other (unplanned) at three different times! One day, Mom wanted some okra, so I ran up the street to the neighborhood grocery store for her, and on my way home, I saw his cousin's mom on her porch. And since his cousin and I were close friends from kindergarten, I knew his mom, too. So, I pulled the car up, ran up to the porch, hugged her, and asked how she was doing and we talked for a little bit... and then, just as I was about to leave, Marvin, his cousin, and his cousin's wife pulled up. Nothing was planned. But in my heart, I asked the Lord if He was trying to tell me something?!

I had prayed the week before, that God would send me a husband. Of course, that wasn't the only time I had prayed that prayer, but this was the season that God was beginning to answer it! After that prayer, I came across the scripture in Isaiah 54:5a NKJV;

> *"For your Maker is your husband; the Lord of hosts is His name."*

After I read that scripture, I was a little stunned, but I said, "Yes, Lord, but become physical. I would like a physical husband that you are in." I prayed that prayer, not asking the Lord Himself to be that man, of course... but expressing my desire for a man filled with God's Spirit. God is my witness; this happened! And that's not all that happened.

Things started manifesting (not manifesting in a new-age way), but God started bringing things to pass, and His word came alive to me several times! And in that same season of prayer, later that week, I prayed and asked the Lord, "Father, please give me a husband that loves you first, and loves me, and serves you with all his heart, and allows me to serve you with all of mine, without hindrance... and Lord, let him be tall, dark, and handsome, and let me be able to relate to him in the natural," (meaning, let him look good to me Lord)! Yes, I sure did pray that prayer! Smiles! Again, I was just being honest! And right after that prayer, a wonderful thing happened: the Holy Ghost brought this scripture to my spirit, as if He were talking to me... because He was (through His word!) and said,

> "*What things soever you desire when you pray, believe that you receive them, and you shall have them.*"
>
> — MARK 11:24 KJV

My spirit reached out and grabbed the spirit of that word... and I believed it, and I received it! The Lord, through His word, said that I shall have it, and He brought His word to pass in my life!! As asked, not only did Marvin and I serve the Lord together without hindering one another for our almost 41 years of marriage... he loved me dearly, and I loved him truly as well! And, to put it bluntly... he was fine!! Just like I asked!

Now, going back to the okra from the store story, I ran up, hugged his cousin's mom, and was just about to leave when they pulled up. We were all so happy to see each other again and greeted one another. We talked with his cousin's mom on the porch for about 15 minutes and then decided to go inside and pray before we all were going to depart. That was kind of a thing back then with us as young adults at that time (we were around 24 years old or so); we would pray together after we finished fellowshipping. The young people did that when I lived in California, too, and a lot of us who went to the church in Denver did that as well (so it wasn't a location thing; it was a Spirit of the Lord thing!).

Once we finished praying, we all were talking with each other... Me and Brother Boyd happened to be talking, and he asked me what I would be doing next. I said I was returning to Texas, and my friend was going with me to visit also, and that I had a little house there... but I told him I was working on my transportation to get back there (and what I didn't tell him was that I felt led to give the money in the offering, that I had planned to use to return home). It wouldn't have been wise to give it; if I hadn't felt led because it was for a need. But I did feel led, and God was in it because Marvin said that he was going toward Texas, and he said he could take us back there. Wow, that was so nice of him, and I was so excited! I thanked him and wanted to tell my friend, so I went into the kitchen to use the phone (this was before cell phones). I called my friend and was about to tell her what Brother Boyd had said... so I said to her, "I was talking to Brother Boyd, and he said..." Then my friend blurted out, "You and Brother Marvin gettin married!" Just like that! Not getting, but gettin married :-) And I was so stunned that she would say that, so I asked her, "What possessed you to say that?!" (Smiling!) She said, "Kathy, it's been on me all week, and I just had to get it out!" Wow! And the funny thing was, even though she was my friend, I had said nothing to her about him before this! I was floored, and my head was spinning (so to speak)... I said, "Lord, this is so real... is this you?!" I was really being careful now, after going through all the brokenness I had gone through before this!

The Lord used circumstances and people close to us to confirm things. Things were happening, and Marvin even saw my parents at a gas station one day during this season of things. They told me, and he told me... and the thing is, my dad was his teacher in middle school... so they knew one another well! Wow! God was working even back then! Even while life was happening to both of us!

Anyway, I told my friend that Bro. Boyd was willing to take us to Texas. I told her that's what I was going to say. So, after we hung up, I went into the bathroom and was so overjoyed.

Man, I was almost floating. I was asking the Lord, what was going on?! Then I felt all this love (not lust) for Marvin, and I said, "Lord, I love him so much." Something was truly happening. And (as a side note, Marvin told me after we got married) that he went in that same bathroom that same day and felt so much love for me, too. He said that God was dealing with him about me, at that time, as well!

I thought about this: it's not a scripture, but someone once said, "My love for God, and his love for God, brought us together!" And sure enough, that's exactly what happened: God's love! And then, the beautiful thing is if you're already married, God's love in you and God's love in your husband can keep you together! Even if the other person doesn't have God's love in them like that, God is able to bless them. Had I known all this during my first marriage... we might have made it. Nonetheless, I'm glad the Lord blessed me with Marvin! But these principles are still very important.

So please don't give up on your marriage; do everything you can do to make it work! I tried to do all I could, (from what I knew), to save my first marriage. So, if it doesn't work after all of that... you can make it! Don't give up on yourself or your future! Stay encouraged!! Trust God, no matter what! He loves you and is concerned about you!!

I kept running into Marvin; I ran into him at the hospital. I was going to visit and pray for my friend there (whom I told you about), and he showed up to pray for her, too. Then, another friend and I went to his cousin's wife to give her some maternity clothes from my friend who had just had her baby. And while we were there, right before we were about to leave, here comes Marvin and his cousin. It was something, like for sure, God was definitely dealing with me/us.

And so again, we were all fellowshipping until my friend and I were going to go on and leave, and they said they were going out to eat and that we could come if we wanted to. And I said, "No, thank you, I'm going home,"... but then I had a quick unction within and changed my mind (which wasn't like me, because I wasn't a wishy-washy type of person). So, I tried to talk my friend into going too. But she didn't want to go. So, it just happened to be me, Marvin, his cousin, and his cousin's wife who were going. Let me say this... what God has for you is for you! Nothing and nobody can stop it, not even the devil!! But remember, you've got to work with your faith... and Faith Works by Love!!

We went to Denny's, ate, and fellowshipped. Marvin was going to drive me home because my friend had driven me to his cousin's earlier, so I didn't have my car. But before that, we ended up back at his cousin's place. Remember his cousin and I were good friends, so I talked with him about how I was feeling and expressed to him what was going on. And he said, "God was dealing with Marvin and confirming a lot, too, so tell him how you feel." All this was really something because I knew how to date, but this was different.

It was a holy matrimony. God was bringing us together in holiness... and getting us ready for a great work together! And the Lord was doing something very real and precious, and people close to us were witnessing it along with us! Another one of my close friends saw me do a cartwheel because I was so happy! Smile's! So anyway, Marvin took me home, and again, in the car, we pulled up in front of my house and started talking.

He started telling me that God had been dealing with him. One of the testimonies he gave me was that since he had been married before, too, and they hadn't seen one another in years, so he wasn't sure if his divorce was final, and one day, right before our talk, he needed to find out. He mentioned that he was at his mother's house, and he asked his mom if she had his ex-wife's phone number. While she was looking for the number, he was sitting in the living room with the phone on his lap, and the phone rang;

he answered it, and it happened to be his ex-wife. He hadn't talked with her in years! And the likelihood of him being at his mother's home at that time (because he didn't live there), and he had just asked his mom for her number, and then she called; he felt that this was orchestrated by the Lord; so that he would know; and do things right. Anyway, she asked how he was doing, and he said he was doing good, and he asked her how she was, and she was good.

After the small talk, she said, "I just want to let you know; you're a free man; the divorce is final." He said, "I was just now trying to find your number to see about that." So, he shared that with me, which was one of the signs and wonders God showed him while He was being dealt with. And his cousin, who flows in the prophetic, also confirmed the will of God. I say confirmed it because prophecy should never be someone just giving you direction for your life. God will deal with you first and then 'confirm' things through a prophet or prophecy that He's already directing you in, or dealing with you about. Don't get that twisted, because, in this day and time, some people are controlling other people through so-called prophecy... and that's not God!

Marvin also told me that one day he was talking to his cousin and told him, "Man, the Lord is dealing with me about a sister." His cousin said, "I know who it is, man." Marvin asked, "Who?!" His cousin answered, "Sister Kathy." He said, "How'd you know?!" And his cousin said, "The Lord showed me that's your wife, man." Again, his cousin only confirmed what God was already dealing with Marvin about.

Just like my friend confirmed what God was already starting to deal with me about—concerning him. I also remembered that the Lord let Marvin see my ex-husband all the way in Dallas (he knew him too, but that was unplanned also)... and out there, Marvin found out that we weren't married anymore. And that was a while before Marvin even saw me in Denver... and he didn't even know that he was going to see me again! Remember, nothing was planned... but the plan of God!! He also told me that he had gone through so much, that he said he told the Lord he was through, and that God would have to hit him in the head with a woman! He said to me, "I guess the Lord let me find my rib, and practically knocked me upside the head with you!" To God only be the Glory! Only JESUS!!!

Anyway, after he shared, he asked me how I felt, and I said, "I feel like the Lord is dealing with me concerning you also." And I shared some signs with him that the Lord had sent me concerning him also. So, we talked a bit, and he said, "Well, now that we know it's God's will for us to be married, we'll pray concerning when and how." I agreed, and we prayed before I got out of the car, and the rest is history!!! And even though we knew God's will for our lives, Marvin wanted to be respectful to my father in the tradition of asking him for the honor of marrying his daughter, and Dad gave him his blessing! After that, Marvin got with me, went down on one knee, and asked me if I would marry him (in respect to me, and tradition as well!) And I said yes! Some traditions are good traditions!

So, we decided to get married before he left for his

upcoming revival, which was scheduled for August 15th, and we were married on August 14, 1978. Remember, July 10, 1978, was when the revival in Denver started?! So, it took God a little over a month to bring us together! The Lord did the confirming, and we did the praying and accepting the will of God, all within that month... and four days later, we were married! His cousin went ahead and started the revival in Arkansas on the first night, and then we drove there to close it out.

We continued running revivals for years and years after that! Praise God!! Within our 41 years of marriage we were blessed with four wonderful sons, two beautiful daughters-in-law, 10 precious grandsons, and three cute granddaughters!!

Thank God, and Hallelujah to Jesus!!! We preached out and established three churches and ministered to and helped drug addicts, dealers, pimps, prostitutes, homosexuals, and gang bangers. Thank God we preached and blessed teachers, business professionals, medical professionals as well, and also just beautiful everyday people who loved the Lord, and some beautiful souls who didn't even know God at one time! We saw people get saved, some were healed, and many were delivered!! To God be the glory for the great things He has done!!

I can honestly say that Marvin (Evangelist Boyd, Pastor Boyd, and Apostle Boyd), not to compare... but in my estimation, was one of the greatest preachers and teachers in the world, in our society at the time (that I knew of). Praise God!! And many people said the same thing! He truly fed us the word of God and made it plain... the word was dynamic through him, he was a powerful preacher (and a great teacher of the word also), our whole marriage! And he was serious with God and loved the Lord impeccably! Marvin held the ministry in high regard and did not play with God, God's word, or God's people!!

He loved, honored, and adored me, and though my man was "bad to the bone" in his work... he didn't put his work/ministry before me. And when I was praying for a husband, and had asked the Lord to not let us hinder one another... I never got in Marvin's way either, when it came to the things of God or the people of God. We dearly loved and were crazy about all of our children, (and I still deeply love them)! And we were so proud of each of them!! He/we also deeply love our grandchildren!! He treated people with kindness and respect! I saw him behind closed doors, and he wasn't a hypocrite at all! What you saw, was what you got! And he was real with God! No, not perfect, but faithful!! Just like the prophecy my Jewish sister in Tulsa said, "God is sending you a husband, and he shall be Faithful to the LORD! The Lord graced me to have a jewel indeed! He was the greatest pastor that I ever had! And I had great pastors! Even though I pastored and served in ministry with Marvin for years and years... he was also an awesome and a wonderful man!! And I thank God for allowing me the time and space to be in this great man's life, and he in mine!! From the broken places to the grace of being humbled and honored, only because of the love of Christ... and through His mercy was this even possible!! And through it all, I learned to trust in Jesus, and the Lord truly proved to be Real, Wonderful, and Faithful! He sure knows how to pick 'em!

And I can say from experience, you can most definitely

trust Him! Because He's good like that!!! What He's done for others, He will do for you... if that's His will for you or whatever His will is, He will and can bless you!! He brought me from brokenness, almost literally being destroyed... to being Dearly Beloved/Well Loved by JESUS, my husband, my family, and many others!! And He will graciously do that for anyone!! Only believe!! Because faith works... if you work it by love! He will bless you according to His will, His way, and His plan for 'you'!! Yes, BELIEVE and Receive!!

I do want to add a very important point concerning having a former marriage. I wanted to make sure that I was doing the right thing before God. Was it alright to be married again, or was it a sin to proceed and get married again? Because some Churches said it was a sin to get married again after a divorce, and some Churches said it wasn't. But I wanted to really understand what God's word said about it. I prayed and prayed about it, and then I decided to speak with a few pastors concerning it, so I could make sure I was in the word of God concerning any decision I might make.

I knew what different scriptures said, and I say a few pastors because I wanted to get their perspectives according to the will of God and His word. The Bible in Proverbs 24:5-6 AMP. says,

> *"A wise man is strong, and a man of knowledge strengthens his power; for by wise guidance, you can wage your war, and in an abundance of [wise] counselors, there is victory and safety."*

So, I spoke with three different pastors at different times and one dear friend. The three pastors had different things to say—some were in the Bible, and some were their professional opinions.

And my dear friend said something to me that stuck... she said, "Kat, wouldn't God want you to be happy?" That made so much sense to me! And yes, He would want us happy, so I wanted to make sure I was in His will according to any happiness that He had for me. And the things that the three pastors said, I respected them and their time and weighed their viewpoints according to the scriptures. And then, finally, I decided that God wasn't saying that I couldn't marry again, and He did want me to be happy according to whatever His will was for me! So, thank God I was free to make the decision to marry, and thank God I have been truly happy because of that decision!

The decision was a blessing, and God knew we needed all those major confirmations that He gave us because we wanted to do the right thing before Him. I had messed up enough, and I really didn't want to keep making major mistakes... I must say that I did repent (ask God for forgiveness many times; and was sorry for the divorce I had). So, of course I'm not saying that divorcing is the right thing all of the time. Each person has to make their own decisions about things because we will each stand before God one day for the decisions we make. We really need to do all we can to do the right thing concerning ourselves, people, and especially according to the word and will of God.

CHAPTER 3

Healing Transforms

Even though a lot of healing had taken place in my life, and the Lord delivered me in so many wonderful ways, my husband helped heal me in that healing process also, and I helped to heal him as well... because we accepted one another as we were. I shared things about my past with him, which he most definitely needed to know, and he shared his with me.

There was a bond of trust, but we still had to do our individual work. I'm still discovering myself, and I remain honest with God. I learned to forgive myself and others, and I am still working on that as well because we have to continue to forgive.

We forgive people because Mark 11:25 MSG. says,

> "If you have anything against someone, forgive---only then will your Heavenly Father be inclined to also wipe your slate clean of sins."

And we have to forgive ourselves, too. If we don't give ourselves grace, like we give others grace, we won't grow. You must give grace and receive it yourself, and then the spiritual steps you take—prayer and meditation on God's word are what will get you through it, and sometimes fasting... and if you need counseling and therapy, get that too. Take good care of yourself; because you are valuable, and you have great significance. And though we are valuable and of great significance and value to God, we still need a Savior and a wonderful Lord... of which He is both. And He makes things alright; when we trust Him!!

I realized I was a broken vessel, a broken person that needed Jesus. I needed healing. I needed wholeness, and I kept praying about it and believing God's word... And He answered many of my prayers. And He continues working things out for me as I allow Him to; and will continue to bless in many ways. Though life may happen, I'd rather it would happen with Jesus in my life, than He not being here. And if life happens, *"He's a very present help in times of trouble."* —Psalm 46:1 (paraphrased).

Healing continued in our lives, even after we got married... and some healing came through each other. Sometimes, we were vulnerable with each other and yet loved one another with God's help, despite the ugly that was still there. Yes, sometimes we went through problems with each other, but always came through those struggles, and it was not always with flying colors either, but because of love, faith, and even when forgiveness was needed, through the tears...we survived and continued to trust in God, and love one another, even if it was sometimes fractured for a moment (a while). Thank God we made it. And, I never disrespected my husband's manhood, or made him feel less than a man. Nor did he ever disrespect me as his wife! And no matter how upset I might have been with him throughout our marriage, (having all sons)... I never disrespected him as a man or decapitated him in front of my sons, nor was I childish; to my sons... (who were growing up to be men). I didn't talk about my husband's faults to them, or to any of my family members... EVER! Nor did he! Sometimes we don't realize that when we talk to our children about our mates faults, we're preparing them to be disrespected in the same manner... by their spouses, and take it! It can cause a form of emotional and psychological abuse toward them, (setting them up to take that kind of abuse). So we really have to be careful not to carry this curse into the next generation (especially since that next generation is still ours... through our children!). Break the curse, and stop the insanity!!

After my husband went Home to be with Jesus, I found this note on Labor Day in 2019 he had left it on our dining room counter. I don't think it was intentional because there were other things on the counter, too. But it was as if this was sitting over to the side by itself. His brief-case was close by, and some of the Manuscripts of his Books that he had been working on were there as well. I left everything right there for a good while because I just didn't have the strength to start looking through it all and organizing it.

Then, one day, as I was walking by it, I picked up this note (and it happened to be on Labor Day in 2019 when I picked it up). Ironically, the date he had written the note to himself was on Labor Day 10 years before this. The reason

I knew it was 10 years before was because on the top of the note, in black ink, it said, "Labor Day," and up the side of the note, in red ink, it said, "31 years of Marriage" (and I found it ten years later; after our 41st Anniversary would have been in 2019). Unfortunately, Marvin had passed away right before our 41st Anniversary. But, the Lord, let me find the note that confirms what I'm sharing with you about love and helping to heal each other. I now keep the note in my wallet, and a couple of my sons have confirmed it's Pop's writing. The words are in all caps, but I'm just going to share the words so as not to seem like I'm tooting my own horn... in red ink also, his note read, "Kathy knows me. She knows my imperfection (I kept the "s" off the end of imperfections because he didn't have it on there), my mistakes, my flaws, my contradictions (he didn't properly say "and") uses "Agape" to love me anyway." The totality of what he said was, "Kathy knows me, she knows my imperfections, my mistakes, my flaws, my contradictions, and uses "Agape" to love me anyway." I praise God!! That's how we do it, with God's Love (Agape)... His love is the only way we can love and help to heal!

    "God is love."

— 1 JOHN 4:8B KJV

And the other forms of love are also important in a relationship; "philia" (affectionate brotherly love), "storge" (familial love), and "eros"(passion)... but Agape should be the foundation of our love in any relationship, "the greatest of these"... because it is God's love.

Pray, read, and study God's word. You don't have to be a scholar or a theologian. Just read the Bible daily. Some of us will go into deeper study for various reasons. Some of us are called to teach the word, so we must *"study to show ourselves approved unto God, a workman that needs not to be ashamed, rightly dividing the word of truth,"* as found in 2 Timothy 2:15 (paraphrased). With all of this; prayer, meditation, and scripture study, it helps in our transformation, and it helps in our renewal, as well as in our deliverance and healing. God's word is spirit and life; Jesus said,

"Every word I've spoken to you is a Spirit-word, so it is life-making."

— JOHN 6:63B MSG

And sometimes transformation happens suddenly, sometimes it happens in a process, and sometimes it happens within both! But it can happen... just BELIEVE!!

And if it's hard to believe, I know it was hard for me to know how to believe at the beginning of my relationship with the Lord, but I asked Him to help me to believe and to know how to yield. He did and will do the same for you if you are struggling in that way. But it is a must to continue working on our relationship with Jesus because we will stand before Him one day... and "no doubt" this is the most important thing in the world we can do... because it's for our Eternity!!!

CHAPTER 4

The Blessing of Love

What I've shared with you has helped me in my personal life and spirit, particularly in my growth in the Lord. You can apply these same truths to your present relationship. Just because you're going through or have been in difficult situations does not mean he isn't your husband or she isn't your wife. If you are married, keep working on things... These are some tools and principles that may help you.

Even though I was blessed and overjoyed to have been given the gift of my husband, Marvin... and to me, there's no one better for me... I might have been able to save my first marriage and avoid all the drama and pain I endured before God gave Marvin to me. But I'm grateful for this promise,

> *"And we know [with great confidence] that God [who is deeply concerned about us] causes*

all things to work together [as a plan] for good
for those who love God, to those who are called
according to His plan and purpose."

— ROMANS 8:28 AMP

He's not a God of divorce and doesn't want us to divorce unless it's a hopeless situation, like abuse or unfaithfulness that won't stop, etc. And you're doing everything you can to make it work, and your husband needs to do the same... even as I mentioned earlier, go to counseling and/or therapy if you all must... and stand. And after doing everything you can, whatever happens at that point... let the Lord guide you from there.

Remember, we must be born again, which includes being renewed and redeemed. Ask Jesus to come into your heart and let Him know you believe in Him and in what He did for you by dying for your sins and God raising Him from the dead for your justification; and total, eternal, and lasting victory!! He's listening to you... and then ask Father God to fill you with His precious Holy Spirit, and He will! That's being born again by faith, and if you can get baptized in water, please do! Acts 2:38 NKJV says,

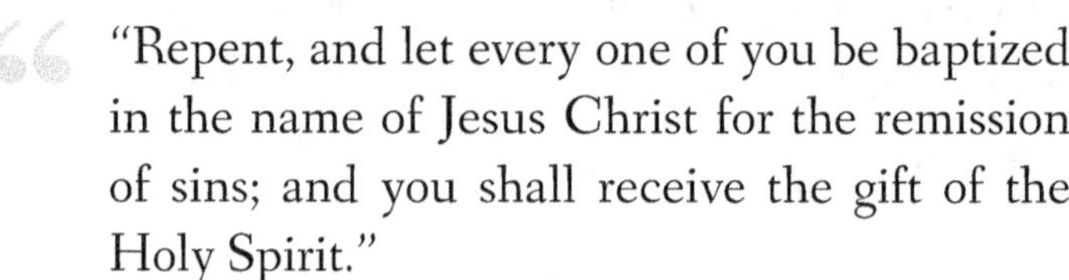

"Repent, and let every one of you be baptized in the name of Jesus Christ for the remission of sins; and you shall receive the gift of the Holy Spirit."

And you may not feel any different, but you may. Just remember, faith is not by feelings; it's by believing and receiving... accepting, saying yes! And that's "The Blessing of Love!"

CHAPTER 5

Faith's Life

After confirming that we believed God brought us together and got married, we knew that we shared the same faith and values. We had challenges, too, but they didn't break us because,

> "a threefold cord is not quickly broken."
>
> — ECCLESIASTES 4:12B KJV

And Jesus was our third cord!! We experienced illnesses, lack at times, betrayal of so-called friends, and more, but we overcame most of it (though not all). At times, we had disagreements with one another, and sometimes, it felt like we had fallen out of love for a season here and there. But like an old couple once said, when asked how they stayed together so long (some of them for 50 and 60 years), and some agreed... "We just didn't fall out of love at the same time!" Epic!

Also, both husband and wife need to be good forgivers because forgiveness will need to be given in any relationship and to be received as well; because we all are imperfect people and can make many mistakes (especially in a marriage!). We must remember God's word says,

> *"Whenever you stand praying if you have anything against anyone, forgive him (or her)... drop the issue, let it go, so that your Father who is in Heaven will also forgive you your transgressions and wrongdoings [against Him and others]. But if you do not forgive, neither will your Father in Heaven forgive your transgressions."*

— MARK 11:25-26 AMP

So, keep the faith. Faith will get you through it. Remember faith's definition:

> *"Faith is the substance of things hoped for, the evidence of things not seen."*

— HEBREWS 11:1 KJV

In another translation, it's said a different way, but with the same meaning, it says,

> *"The fundamental fact of existence is that this trust in God, this faith, is the firm foundation*

under everything that makes life worth living. It's our handle on what we can't see."

— HEBREWS 11:1 MSG

And one last translation,

"Faith is the assurance (title deed, confirmation) of things hoped for (divinely guaranteed), and the evidence of things not seen [the conviction of their reality— faith comprehends as fact what cannot be experienced by the physical senses]."

— HEBREWS 11:1 AMP

CHAPTER 6

Dearly Beloved

Marvin loved me in spite of me, and I loved him in spite of him. Before and during our marriage, I shared deep and embarrassing things with him, and to my surprise, he still loved me. He did things that weren't perfect, and I still loved him.

We were continuing to be healed. And we were truly loved (Dearly Beloved)! Our love for God and each other added children and grandchildren to our lives... and multiplied as we ministered to others, loving and blessing their lives and families as well!

Our oldest son is a dear-hearted, anointed, dynamic spoken word artist and a prolific musician in his own right. He and his beautiful, truly blessed, dear, and honorable wife are a loving couple who have three wonderful, respectful, dedicated, and smart sons!

Our second son is overcoming challenges through his faith with a dear, precious, loving, and great heart... and he has beautiful, wonderful, kind, and precious children as well!

Our third oldest son served our Country well and is a Retired Sergeant in the Army... and is a very nice, strong and successful businessman extraordinaire... with a dearly precious, wonderful, smart, and lovely wife. They both are dynamic life and business partners, making significant impacts together. And they have three of the cutest, sweetest, smartest, and happiest children ever!

Our youngest son is a viable and focused entrepreneur, managing his finances well. He is smart, determined, dedicated, steady, and solid! And all of them love the Lord and work and minister to bless their family, as well as others' lives! Each one is a prayer warrior/intercessor indeed, and if need be, they can cast the devil out if they see him hurting someone they love! Glory to JESUS!!! And even their children can pray, and quite a few of them know and speak God's word!!

So, I can truly say little did I know what God had planned for my life; in bringing me from brokenness to being Dearly Beloved... truly loved by our wonderful Heavenly Father, my awesome Lord and Savior Jesus Christ, our precious Holy Ghost... and loved by a dear man, and great man of God, my husband, Marvin!! God brought us together within five weeks and kept us together for almost 41 years!! And blessed our life, our family, our work, and our ministry!! No, it all wasn't a perfect life, or a perfect marriage, or a perfect family, and we weren't perfect people... we were just blessed by the grace of a Perfect God!!

And, this doesn't mean that everyone should come

together the way we did... let God lead you individually; dating for a while can be a good thing, there are benefits to dating for a period of time. Sometimes, people may date for six months or a year or more before they get married, and they can also have a wonderful marriage. Whatever works for you. Also, every man that God blesses a woman with doesn't have to be a preacher for him to be a good man. He can be a good man if he doesn't preach and do that kind of work. Just loving the Lord, working hard or smart, taking good care of his wife and children, and being in one accord with his woman can also make him a good man. And, the same with women... brother, they don't have to be like me to be a good wife or a good woman... or pray like or as much as me or even more than me. God's hand is on each of us for His purpose, and we all are different. He has different plans for us that are good and powerful in their own way! So, you, be you boo!! And everyone be who God is making you to be, into Christ's image! You all got this... with JESUS!! The word is for everyone, whichever way you need it. These keys and tips are not gender related; they are principle and word-related.

I imagine the Lord said to Marvin, *"Come, my blessed son, enter into your eternal joy with your Lord... well done, my good and faithful servant!!"* Matthew 25:21 (paraphrased). And, I am so blessed to have partnered with such a wonderful man, and a great man of God, in all these beautiful gifts... and even through the hard times, we made it! Praise God!! And we had really great and the best of times too!! We saw hundreds of people blessed through our lives and ministry... many were healed and delivered like us! We did good! Only by His grace!! Hallelujah! And honey, I will see you later! I'll always love you, man of God... you are my heart and my Forever Brother!!

TO MY WONDERFUL AND GRACIOUS HEAVENLY FATHER!!! YOU ALONE ARE WORTHY TO BE PRAISED!! ALMIGHTY GOD!!! I PRAISE YOU, GRACIOUS AND SWEET JESUS!!! AND HOLY GHOST... PRECIOUS SPIRIT OF GOD, YOU ARE GREAT AND DEAR AND POWERFUL AND WONDERFUL DEAR LORD!!! AND I LOVE YOU ALL WITH ALL MY HEART AND SOUL!! THANK YOU SO VERY, VERY MUCH FOR WHO YOU ARE AND FOR ALL THAT YOU HAVE DONE, AND CONTINUE TO DO!!!

LOVINGLY! Your Daughter, Kathy

Afterword

As I reflect on all the Lord has done for me and where He's brought me from, I can't help but have a heart full of gratitude and gratefulness! He's been with me through it all, from the moment Jesus came into my heart in my car, with all His lovingkindness, graciousness, and forgiveness... to realizing who He is, to receiving the precious Gift of the Holy Ghost and His loving greatness and power!! I couldn't have been more blessed! Not because I'm so great, but because I was a sinner in need of a Savior, and my Lord was there for me! With all the love and forgiveness that I needed, every step of the way... all the way, and He's still here!! Thank you, Lord!!

And I want to encourage you, dear sister, brother, and friend, to stay encouraged. No matter what you're going through, believe God! And know that you are Dearly Beloved as well!! Not because you are perfect, but because you are you! He loves you for you!! You don't have to be anything or anyone but yourself, with all your imperfections and flaws, like me... our Heavenly Father truly loves us! Continue to hope and believe that no matter what you're going through, you can make it, and He will help you with those imperfections and flaws and heal, as well as deliver you! *"He perfects that which concerns you!"* — Psalm 138:8a, (paraphrased). Stand strong, even though you may be falling or even failing. Stand strong in faith!! God got you!!

And He will make you what He wants you to be! Whole!! Trust and ask Him for that!!

And in spite of your weaknesses and imperfections, open your heart to the possibility of divine love and blessings. And know this: Jesus is here for you, and His Salvation is ready to save and heal you!! And real love (Jesus) can and will deliver you!! And He has perfect love for you and will see you through everything!! Know that, *"There is no fear in love. But perfect love drives out fear, because fear has to do with punishment. The one who fears is not made perfect in love."* —1 John 4:18 NIV. Only believe! He will help to bring you out of everything He sees fit... just call on HIS Name!! And trust His LOVE for You, for you are Dearly Beloved!!! JESUS is coming soon! GET AND STAY READY!!!

Much love, peace, grace, and blessings!!!

In HIM!
Love, Kathy

P.S. Say this Prayer, in your own way... "Thank

you, **FATHER GOD**, for loving me; and sending **JESUS CHRIST** to die for my sins! Jesus, please forgive me for all my sins, come into my heart, and save my soul. Help me to believe, and fill me, Father, with your precious **HOLY SPIRIT**. *In Jesus Name!* **AMEN!!**

"How to Be Led by The Holy Spirit"

"The Need to Hear from God"

"The Power of the Resurrection" (God's Act of War)

"History is HIS-Story" (The True Meaning and Beauty of Christmas; Without taking the joy of loving others out of it.)

And there are many more of mine and my Husband's Works or Books... So stay tuned!!

Our Books will be Hardcover Books, Paperback Books, AudioBooks, and/or Ebooks!!

For Orders go to; BoydMinistries.Org

Also look for our Books online at Amazon, Walmart, and Barnes & Noble, etc.

Contact Information:

Kathy King-Boyd (Boyd Ministries)

2590 Welton St. #200-1198

(571) 281-2901

KingsDaughter@BoydMinistries.Org

And if you are going through abusive situations, please get some help. I could have eventually been killed, but thank God I got out before that.

Google for **HELP**

Google for good **CHURCHES**

Here are some phone numbers to possibly get assistance. I do not know of these personally, I looked up these numbers so you can possibly get some information here, (so I do not take responsibility to know of the help, nor do I have personal knowledge of these supposed Resources).

And for help or assistance in other areas of your life, (i.e. food, clothing, shelter/housing, jobs, etc.), you can possibly contact "United Way" in your area.

National Domestic Violence Hotline; (800) 799-7233

Text BEGIN to 88788

National Sexual Assault Hotline

Hours: Available 24 hours; (800) 656-4673

If in a Mental Health Crisis, call 988!

God bless you!! Please seek help if you need it! You are loved!!

~

Find a good church, a great pastor, that preaches the word of God, teaches about the Holy Spirit, and is a church that God's love flows through.

Remember there is no perfect church, because there are no perfect people… just loving people, trying to know and serve a perfect and loving God!

~